D0870051

WHY DOES MY BODY SMELL?

✦ and other questions about hygiene ✦

Angela Royston

Heinemann Library
Chicago, Illinois

Customer Service 888-454-2279
Visit our website at www.heinemannlibrary.com

Designed by Joanna Sapwell and StoryBooks
Illustrations by Nick Hawken
Originated by Ambassador Litho
Printed by South China Printers, Hong Kong

07 06 05 04 03
10 9 8 7 6 5 4 3 2 1

Library of Congress Cataloging-in-Publication Data
Royston, Angela.
  Why does my body smell? : and other questions about hygiene / Angela
Royston.
      p. cm. -- (Body matters)
Includes index.
Summary: Answers common questions about hygiene.
  ISBN 1-40340-208-6 (HC)   ISBN 1-40340-463-1 (PB)
  1. Hygiene--Juvenile literature. [1. Cleanliness. 2. Health.] I.
Title. II. Series.
  RA780 .R696 2002
  613'.4--dc21
                          2002003549

Acknowledgments
The author and publishers are grateful to the following for permission to reproduce copyright material:
pp. 4, 9, 13, 18, 23, 24, 27, 28 Science Photo Library; pp. 5, 6, 8, 10, 14, 15, 16, 17, 19, 22, 25, 26 Gareth Boden; p. 7 Action Plus; p. 12 Trevor Clifford; p. 20 Powerstock Zefa; p. 21 Willibie Animal Photography.

Cover photograph by Gareth Boden.

Some words are shown in bold, **like this.** You can find out what they mean by looking in the glossary.

CONTENTS

WHY IS DIRT BAD FOR MY BODY?

Dirt contains millions of **germs** that can make you sick in different ways. Germs are tiny forms of life that are too small to see except through a powerful microscope. They include **bacteria, viruses,** and some kinds of **fungi.**

Bacteria and viruses

Bacteria are very small but they can multiply very fast. They breed fastest of all in warm, damp places, such as in your throat and lungs. Most

Bacteria are so small they have to be magnified at least 1,000 times before you can see them. This kind of bacteria causes sore throats.

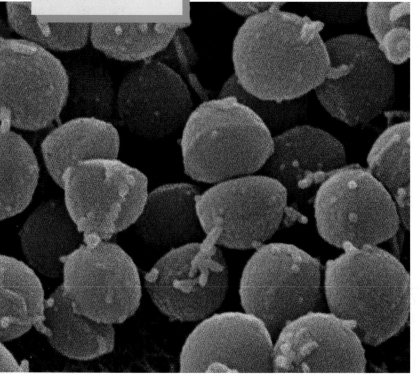

bacteria that live inside your body and on your skin are harmless, but some can make you ill. Dirt often contains those kinds of bacteria. Viruses are even smaller than bacteria. More than 10,000 viruses could fit into the space of the smallest **bacterium.** Different kinds of virus cause different illnesses.

Fungi

There are many kinds of fungi and most of them do not make you sick. Mushrooms and yeast are two kinds of fungi that are good to eat. But some fungi, such as those that cause athlete's foot, attack the body.

SOME ILLNESSES CAUSED BY GERMS

- bacteria: gum disease, upset stomach, conjunctivitis
- viruses: colds, warts, chickenpox, measles, polio
- fungi: athlete's foot, ringworm

Protecting yourself against dirt

Your skin protects most of your body from dirt and germs. Germs cannot get through your skin unless it is cut or scratched. Most get inside your body through your nose or mouth, so it is important to wash dirt and germs off your skin, particularly your hands, before they spread to your nose or mouth.

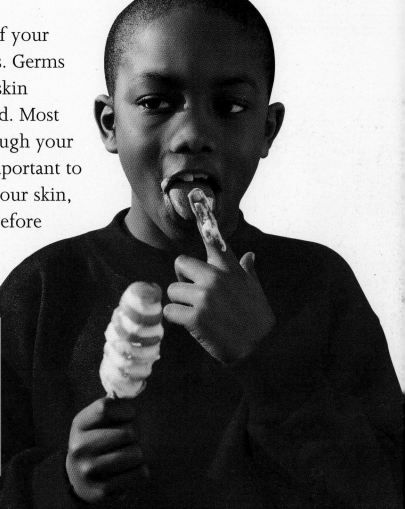

This boy is licking ice cream off his fingers. If his fingers are dirty, germs from his skin will get inside his mouth and into his stomach.

WHY DO MY FEET SMELL?

Feet become smelly when they sweat and the sweat cannot escape into the air. Instead it soaks through your socks and into your shoes. The sweat in your shoes becomes stale and smells. When you wear the shoes again and your feet become hot and sweaty, the smell spreads to your socks and feet. Bare feet never become smelly from sweating.

This girl likes to wear gym shoes all day, but they make her feet smell.

Sweat

Your feet are not the only part of you that sweats. Your body makes almost two pints (one liter) of salty sweat a day. It oozes out all over your skin and you are not usually aware of it. Your body takes in and loses water every day. Sweating is just one of the ways that it loses water. When you are very hot, your body makes extra sweat that makes you feel damp and sticky. As the extra sweat **evaporates** it helps to cool you down. It makes your skin cooler, but it leaves behind a thin layer of salt.

Bacteria

Pure sweat does not usually smell. It smells when bacteria live and breed in it. This happens inside your shoes, between your toes, and under your arms. Bacteria live on the salt and other substances contained in the sweat.

MOST SWEAT

The sweatiest parts of the body are the soles of the feet, the palms of the hands, and the forehead. Sweat can also collect in your armpits.

Exercise makes you hot. The hotter you get, the more you sweat.

Reducing the smell

The best way to stop sweat from smelling is to use soap and water to wash away the stale sweat before bacteria can breed in it. Having a shower or bath every day washes your whole body and stops stale sweat from building up. If you cannot wash your whole body, you should wash the sweatiest parts, such as your feet.

Showering washes away stale sweat and dirt and keeps you smelling clean and fresh.

Clean clothes

Sweat that gathers in socks and other clothes can also become smelly, so change your clothes regularly. If your feet are sweaty you will need to wear clean socks every day. If your shoes are very smelly, it may be possible to wash them too. If your shoes cannot be washed, you can buy special insoles, loose pads that fit inside your shoes, that will help get rid of the smell.

Deodorants

Using **deodorant** is a good way to make sure your sweat does not smell. They contain chemicals that stop the **bacteria** from breeding, and they usually contain a perfume to make your skin smell fresh. Most deodorants are made for using on your armpits.

Antiperspirants

Many deodorants also contain an **antiperspirant** that stops the skin from sweating. But the skin needs to sweat, so, if you use an antiperspirant, make sure that you wash it off before you go to bed. Then your skin can sweat normally again.

This is what skin covered with sweat droplets looks like under a microscope. It contains many sweat glands. They pump salty water out of the body onto the skin.

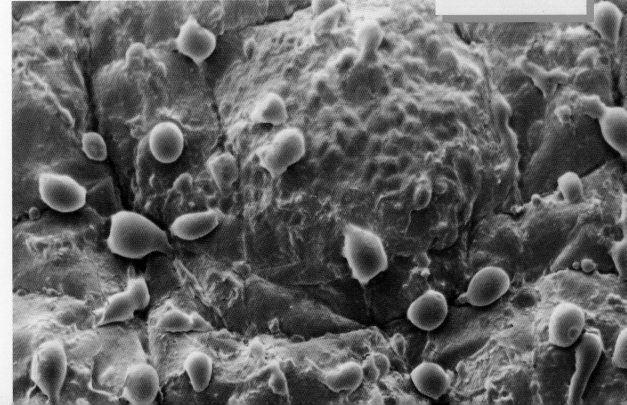

WHY DO I NEED TO BRUSH MY TEETH?

You need to brush your teeth to clean away tiny pieces of food and **bacteria** that cling to your teeth. When you brush your teeth, brush from the gums to the tip of the teeth. Remember to brush the backs of your teeth as well as the fronts. Then brush the tops of the large, flat molar teeth at the back of your mouth.

Teeth under attack

When you eat, tiny pieces of food dissolve in your **saliva** and cling around and between your teeth. Bacteria live and breed in the saliva. As bacteria feed on the pieces of food, especially on sweet, sugary food, they produce a strong **acid.** The acid attacks the **enamel** that covers your teeth. Enamel is the hardest substance in your body, but it is not strong enough to resist the acid. The acid can make a hole, called a cavity, in the enamel. Then it attacks the softer **dentine** below.

Toothpaste contains special chemicals that help to remove food, saliva, and bacteria from the surface of your teeth. It also leaves a fresh, clean taste in your mouth.

Toothache

If a cavity in a tooth is not filled by a dentist, it grows, until it attacks the pulp in the center of the tooth. Then the tooth will begin to hurt badly.

Protecting your teeth

It is important to care for your teeth. The first set of teeth, the baby teeth, fall out between the ages of about five and twelve. The adult teeth that grow to replace them have to last your whole life. You can protect your teeth by brushing them regularly, flossing, and visiting your dentist twice a year.

The inside of a tooth has layers. Underneath the hard enamel is the dentine, which is as hard as bone. A soft pulp is inside the dentine.

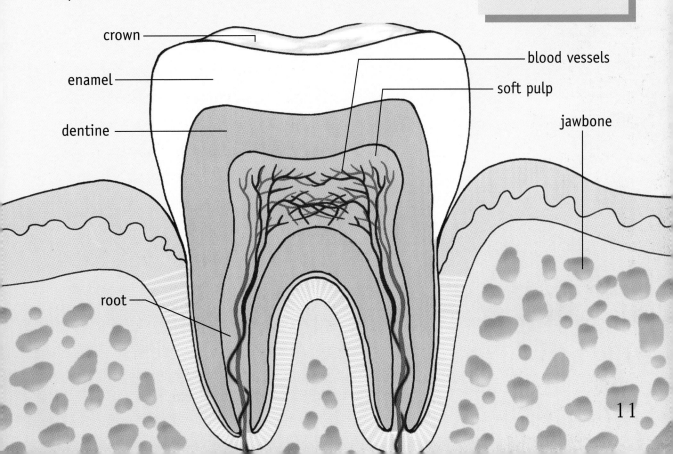

crown

enamel

dentine

root

blood vessels

soft pulp

jawbone

Brushing your teeth

The best way to protect your teeth is to brush them regularly. You should brush them every morning and every evening before you go to bed. It also helps to clean them after eating or drinking anything sweet. If you cannot clean your teeth after eating, a drink of water will help to wash away the pieces of leftover food and **bacteria** in your mouth.

This boy has had a disclosing tablet. It shows how much plaque he has by staining it blue. Now he has to brush his teeth well to brush away the plaque.

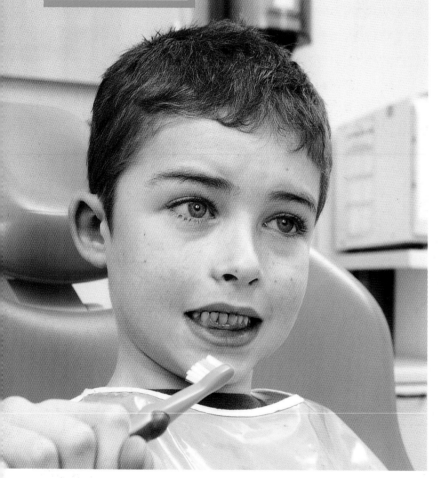

Dental floss

Plaque is a smelly paste that can build up around your teeth and under the edge of your gums. It consists of saliva and bacteria. It is difficult to remove all the plaque with a toothbrush. Dental floss is a thin string that you pull between your teeth and under the edge of your gums to remove any plaque that has built up there.

Dental check-ups

Dentists keep your teeth and mouth healthy. The dentist checks your gums and teeth. If a tooth has started to decay he or she will fill it with special chemicals to stop the hole from getting any bigger. The dentist may coat your teeth with a layer of fluoride to protect them from decay.

WHAT IS IN TOOTHPASTE?

Toothpaste is a mixture of glycerol, a thick liquid, and:
- very fine chalk that scrubs your teeth
- a soapy substance that helps to remove dirt
- oil, such as peppermint oil, as a flavor
- a sweetener that contains no sugar

A dentist is using a small mirror and a metal probe to examine all around this child's teeth.

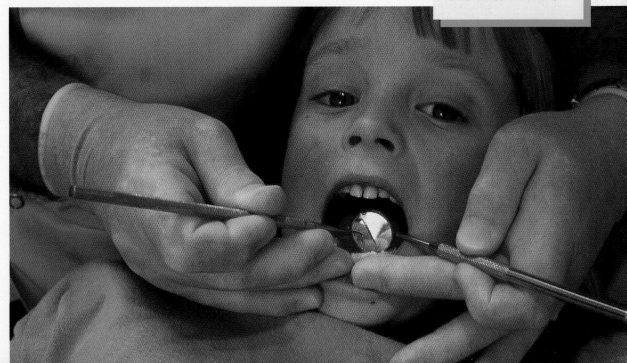

HOW DO GERMS SPREAD?

Illnesses that are passed from one person to another are said to be **infectious.** Some **germs** get inside the body when you breathe in air. Other germs spread to your body because you touch them without realizing it. For example, if someone has an upset stomach they may have germs in their mouth or on their hands. If you drink from the same mug or glass as them, the germs can spread from their mouth onto the mug and then into your mouth.

If you have a cold, always cover your mouth when you cough or sneeze. This way you are less likely to pass on your germs.

Germs in the air

You cannot help breathing in germs—they are in the air all around you. With many illnesses, people breathe out germs with the stale air from their lungs. The germs float through the air and may be breathed in by other people who are nearby. Colds, chickenpox, and measles are caught in this way. When someone coughs or sneezes, millions of extra germs are launched into the air.

By direct contact

Some illnesses are **contagious.** This means
you have to touch the germs to catch them.
Conjunctivitis, for example, makes your eyes
red and swollen. The germs that cause it have to
touch your eyes. This is most likely to happen if
you touch the germs without knowing it and
then rub your eyes. Or you may come into
contact with the germs in a swimming pool. If
one of your friends has conjunctivitis, do not use
his towel to dry your face because you will
probably rub some of his germs into your eyes.

Always use your
own towel to dry
yourself. That way
you are less likely
to pick up other
people's germs
or pass on your
own germs.

15

WHY SHOULD I WASH MY HANDS?

Your fingers and hands pick up germs easily because you touch things all the time. Washing your hands with soap and hot water cleans away the germs.

The best way to stop **germs** from getting into your mouth is to wash your hands before you eat, after going to the bathroom, and after handling pets.

Germs rub off onto your hands and fingers when you touch something that has germs on it. They can easily spread into your mouth when you touch your face. And if you eat something with your fingers, germs can rub off onto the food and pass into your mouth and stomach. Always wash your hands before you eat.

Be careful what you eat

Some food may contain a lot of germs. Fresh fruit and vegetables may have germs on the outside. Always peel or wash fruit and vegetables before you eat them. Be careful about eating food that has not been covered or wrapped. Flies like to settle on trash and on animal droppings, which are full of germs. Some of the germs rub off onto their bodies. If they then land on food that has been left uncovered, they will leave germs on the food.

This girl is hungry but she cannot wash her hands. Instead she is making sure that her fingers do not touch the bar she is eating.

Fighting back

You do not have to protect yourself from every single germ, because your body is very good at fighting them. **Saliva** is slightly antiseptic, so it can kill some of the germs. Although you may swallow the rest, strong **acid** in your stomach will kill them. But, if there are very many germs, they may multiply faster than your body can kill them. When this happens, the germs make you sick.

Germs in the toilet

There are many germs in and around the toilet. They come from feces, the solid waste that you and other people expel into the toilet. Many **bacteria** live naturally in the large intestine. They help to break down food and will not harm you while they remain there. When solid waste leaves your body, many of these bacteria pass out with it. Many spread onto your hands, so make sure you wash your hands after you have gone to the bathroom. If you do not, the germs may get into your mouth and make you ill.

Worms

Sometimes pinworms, or threadworms as they are often called, get inside your intestines and live and breed there. Pinworms are parasites. This means that they feed off your body.

This is a magnified photo of a pinworm. They make your skin itch, especially at night.

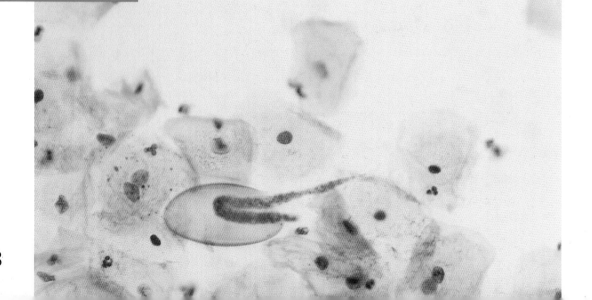

Pinworms are harmless but they make your anus itchy and sore. They usually get inside your body as unhatched eggs that stick to your fingers and under your fingernails. The eggs are too small to see but they still pass into your mouth.

Worms can be cured by taking special medicine. The best way to avoid catching them is to wash your hands after going to the bathroom and before eating.

Washing your hands after going to the bathroom will protect you from catching pinworms.

DON'T BE A SUCKER

Don't put pens, pencils, coins, or anything else in your mouth. You don't know what germs, dirt, or even eggs may be clinging to them!

Pets

Pets have many **germs,** mostly in their mouths and in their droppings. It is nice to pet, pick up, and cuddle pets, but do not let their germs spread to you. The best way to prevent this from happening is to wash your hands after handling animals and after cleaning out their cages.

Pets carry germs on their feet, on their fur, and in their mouths. Wash your hands after handling a pet so that you do not catch their germs.

How animals spread germs

Animals often get into trash and sniff each other's droppings. Do not let dogs lick your face. The **acid** in their stomachs is stronger than the acid in ours, so germs around their mouths do not harm them. The same germs can make us ill. Feathers and fur trap dirt, dust from the animal's own skin, and germs. Although cats are well-known for cleaning themselves, their fur is full of germs. You can help keep your pet's fur clean by brushing and combing it, but do not forget to wash your hands afterwards.

Cleaning out their homes

Small pets such as rabbits, guinea pigs, hamsters, and gerbils are usually kept in hutches or cages. These cages have to be cleaned regularly. You should give the pet fresh bedding material. It is very important to throw away old food, droppings, and other things from the floor of the hutch or cage. Cleaning washes away germs that can make your pet sick and keeps the cage from smelling. Fish tanks and bowls also need to be cleaned regularly to keep the fish that live in them healthy.

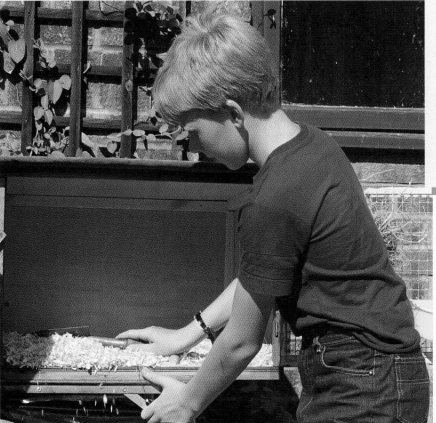

This boy is cleaning out his rabbit's hutch. This will make it more comfortable for the rabbits and healthier for him and for them.

DO ONLY ATHLETES GET ATHLETE'S FOOT?

Athlete's foot usually starts as dry, itchy skin between the toes. Check your feet regularly and always dry them carefully.

Athlete's foot is caused by a **fungus** that usually grows between the toes and on the soles of the feet. It makes the skin itchy and flaky. Everyone who shares a bathroom or walks in bare feet will come into contact with the fungus, but some people catch it more easily than others. The fungus grows well in hot, moist places. It is common on an athlete's feet, which are often hot and sweaty.

Avoiding athlete's foot

Try not to let your feet spend too long in sweaty socks and shoes. Wash carefully between your toes, and dry your feet thoroughly on your own towel. If you use other people's towels you may catch the disease from them. Rubbing talcum powder between the toes helps to make sure they are completely dry.

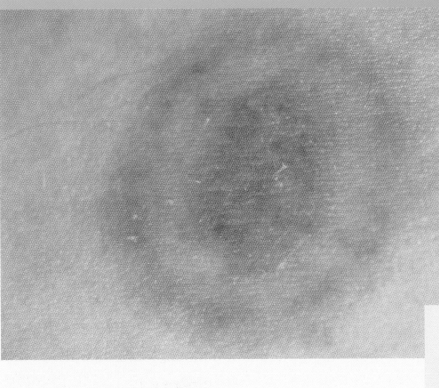

This person is suffering from ringworm. The disease is caused by a fungus and has nothing to do with worms.

Treating athlete's foot

Washing and drying your feet carefully may be enough to get rid of the fungus. If this does not work, you can get a special cream from the pharmacy that will soon cure athlete's foot.

Ringworm

Ringworm is the name given to another skin condition caused by a fungus. Ringworm begins as a small red patch that spreads out. The skin in the middle of the patch heals, leaving a scaly ring that is often itchy. You can get ringworm on most parts of your skin but it is most common on the hands, arms, neck, scalp, and chest. Ringworm is very **infectious** but it is easy to cure by using a special cream.

23

HOW DO YOU CATCH PLANTAR WARTS?

Plantar warts are a kind of wart that forms on the sole of your foot. It is caused by a **virus** that gets into the top layer of skin through a crack, scratch, or scrape. These warts are very **infectious** and spread easily, not only to other people, but also to another part of your foot. You catch them by walking on the virus in bare feet. If a plantar wart is not treated, it can become painful to walk on.

A wart is a bump in the skin. Warts are not very infectious and often disappear as unexpectedly as they appear.

Warts

Like plantar warts, warts are caused by a virus in the top layer of your skin. Each wart contains millions of virus cells. Some of these cells have to get into your skin to infect you. The virus can stay in the skin for months before it develops into one or more warts. The warts appear as small bumps on the skin, usually on the hands or face. They are not very infectious and usually go away on their own, although it may take some time.

HOW TO AVOID SPREADING PLANTAR WARTS:

- do not wear other people's shoes
- shower before and after swimming
- do not use other people's towels
- keep your plantar warts under a watertight covering when you swim.

Treating warts and plantar warts

Pharmacies sell different ointments, or creams, for warts and plantar warts. Many ointments kill the skin around the plantar wart until it falls off. If a plantar wart refuses to go away, a doctor can freeze it off or remove it with a laser.

Plantar warts affect the soles of your feet. You can catch them when you borrow a towel from a friend.

HOW DO YOU GET NITS?

Nits are the empty eggs of head lice. You catch them when a louse crawls into your hair and lays its eggs. Head lice feed by biting your scalp and sucking the blood. They can make your scalp itchy, and this is the most common sign that you are infected. Head lice move fast and pass very easily from one head to another. If one person in a family is infected, everyone in the family will probably be infected too.

Head lice

Head lice can crawl from one head to another, even if the people's heads only touch for a moment.

Each louse lays many tiny eggs, which it sticks to a hair about a centimeter from the scalp. The new, young lice hatch about a week later, but the empty shell, or nit, remains glued to the hair. The young lice feed on your blood

and grow quickly. They start to lay their own eggs after about ten days, so the number of head lice in your hair increases rapidly.

Having head lice is not a sign that you have dirty hair. Head lice like to lay their eggs on clean hair.

Getting rid of head lice

You cannot wash head lice out of your hair with ordinary shampoo. You have to use a special shampoo or other treatment that kills the lice instead. A nit comb has teeth that are very close together. You should use it after treating your hair to comb out the dead lice. Lice spread so easily you cannot avoid them! The best way to stop them is for everyone in your class at school and in your family to treat their hair for lice on the same night.

WHY DO I HAVE REGULAR MEDICAL CHECKUPS?

You need to have a checkup from time to time to make sure that you are generally healthy. A doctor or nurse will measure your height and weight to make sure that you are growing well. Your eyes and ears will be tested to check that they are working properly.

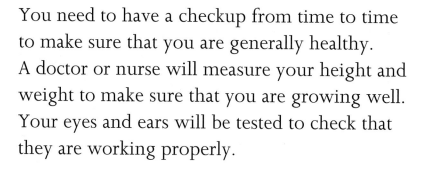

This boy is being measured as part of a medical checkup.

Sight test

When your eyesight is tested you have to read large and small letters from a distance. People who are short-sighted cannot see distant things clearly. Long-sighted people find it difficult to read print in books or on labels. For people with astigmatism, everything may appear slightly blurred. All of these conditions can be corrected with glasses.

Hearing test

If the tubes inside your ears are blocked, you may have trouble hearing until the tubes are unblocked. Some people need a hearing aid to help them hear better.

BODY MAP

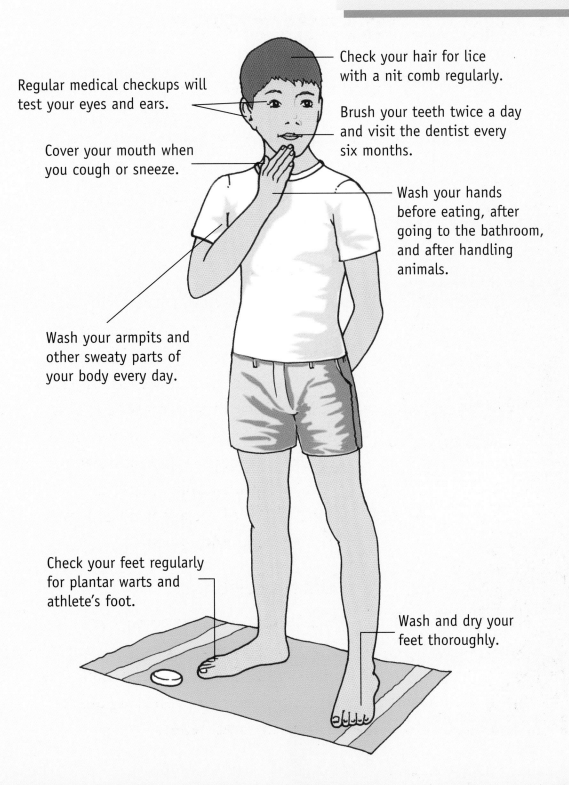

Keep yourself clean and healthy!

Check your hair for lice with a nit comb regularly.

Regular medical checkups will test your eyes and ears.

Brush your teeth twice a day and visit the dentist every six months.

Cover your mouth when you cough or sneeze.

Wash your hands before eating, after going to the bathroom, and after handling animals.

Wash your armpits and other sweaty parts of your body every day.

Check your feet regularly for plantar warts and athlete's foot.

Wash and dry your feet thoroughly.

GLOSSARY

acid   liquid with a sour, bitter taste

antiperspirant   substance applied to the body to stop sweating

bacteria   tiny living things. Some kinds of bacteria are germs that cause disease.

bacterium   single bacteria

contagious   when germs are passed from one person to another, by touching the germs themselves

dentine   part of a tooth below the enamel

deodorant   substance that stops sweat from smelling bad

enamel   very hard substance that covers your teeth

evaporate   turn from water into tiny droplets in the air

fungi   living things that are like plants in many ways but have no green leaves

fungus   one kind of fungi

germs   microscopic forms of life that can make you ill

infectious   when germs that cause illness can be passed from one person to another

plaque sticky coating containing bacteria that builds up on teeth after eating

saliva fluid produced in the mouth that helps in the digestive process

virus kind of germ that is even smaller than all kinds of bacteria

FURTHER READING

McGinty, Alice. *Good Hygiene*. Danbury Conn.: Franklin Watts, 1999.

McGinty, Alice. *Staying Healthy: Good Hygiene*. New York: PowerKids Press, 1997.

Stewart, Alex. *Keeping Clean*. Danbury, Conn.: Franklin Watts, 2000.

Index